Halloween Carving

Paul F. & Camille J. Bolinger

Schiffer Publishing Ltd
4880 Lower Valley Road, Atglen, PA 19310 USA

Dedication

My deepest thanks once more to Camille and Jake. Working at home has its rewards but it also puts a heavy load on the family. My wife and son have both supported me in every new challenge. Thanks and I love you both.

Library of Congress Catalog Card Number: 98-85407

Designed by Laurie A. Smucker
Type set in Times New Roman/University Roman Bd BT

ISBN: 0-7643-0608-1
Printed in China

Published by Schiffer Publishing Ltd.
4880 Lower Valley Road
Atglen, PA 19310
Phone: (610) 593-1777; Fax: (610) 593-2002
E-mail: Schifferbk@aol.com
Please write for a free catalog.
This book may be purchased from the publisher.
Please include $3.95 for shipping.

In Europe, Schiffer books are distributed by
Bushwood Books
6 Marksbury Avenue
Kew Gardens
Surrey TW9 4JF England
Phone: 44 (0) 181 392-8585; Fax: 44 (0) 181 392-9876
E-mail: Bushwd@aol.com

Please try your bookstore first.

We are interested in hearing from authors with book ideas on related subjects.

Acknowledgments

I would like to thank Pat McChesney for his fine photography and his stalwart friendship. The demands on Pat as CEO of his company are enormous but somehow he still manages to make the time to help me with my wacky adventures. There's no one else like you Pat. I know the time you put in here at our studio would normally belong to your family; please thank them for sharing you.

Contents

Introduction

As a professional woodcarver I am also a designer, which means I must continue to come up with new ideas and designs to keep my work fresh and original. Creating new designs involves not only inspiration but also lots of grunt work. This is quite a challenge for anyone but I think it is especially difficult for people like me with no formal art training. Without the formal training, every element of a design must be worked out by whatever means—usually trial and error in my case. Even when the inspiration exists, there are still the challenges of the details and "the devil is in the details."

In this book I have provided five patterns for carvers to get you started, but I have also included quite a few design notes and ideas that I developed while working on Halloween designs. These ideas and notes are the results of both observation of other works and lots of trial and error. Hopefully I have done the trial and error work for the reader, who can then skip on to the fun part.

These notes and ideas try to show how the details of the design can be accomplished to help pull together a complete and appealing design. If I have succeeded, this book will be an invaluable tool for the carver/designer that retains its value for many years.

Chapter One
What Is It About Halloween?

Halloween Night ...

I dressed up so good that I could scare,
all the scary things out there.
So with my bag and a little light
I went out to prowl the night.

I went with haste from door to door
collecting goodies more and more.
Until I found myself alone
and very, very far from home.

As I turned to go on back
I held up my light and lifted my sack.
But from the darkness all about
a cold wind blew my light right out.

Now I'm not an easy one to scare
but horrid things were lurking there;
ghosts and goblins filled the air
and goose bumps helped to raise my hair.

I tried to act like I was brave
but it was dark like in a cave.
I could feel them drawing near
from deep inside rose a terrible fear.

I ran as fast as I could fly
and tried so hard not to cry
until I reached my own front stair
and found my mother waiting there.

I was so glad I shed a tear
and hid in her arms from my deep fear.
But I knew just what her smile must mean,
that I'd go right back out next Halloween.

—Paul F. Bolinger

Halloween is my second favorite holiday because of the kids, the fun, and the memories. At my age the things that scare me out of my wits have nothing at all to do with Halloween but that doesn't mean I can't remember. Perhaps the pleasure of remembering things from childhood, turning them over in your mind and savoring them, is reason enough to do a little Halloween carving. If so, you are in for a double treat since you can have your own memories and make new memories too. There is no doubt others will enjoy the memories you carve when you show, give, or sell your Halloween creations.

I joke that I suffer from SMS (Separated Memory Syndrome), sometimes referred to as CRS (Can't Remember S—), therefore I can't fully trust all my memories of Halloween. Also there are things that happened back in those days I don't want my Mom, Dad, or for that matter my son, to read. What I remember now are the good things. I remember going door to door with a pillow case and coming home with it full of treats—sometimes more than once. My Dad was in the army so, at times, we lived in army housing where there were plenty of doors to knock on. I remember that my older brother was able to hoard his candy so well that he would have a supply of Halloween candy well into the spring of the following year. He kept his candy in a drawer in the bedroom where any of us could get to it. We had long since devoured all of our own but no one dared to take any of his. We were sure he knew where each piece belonged and he was a heck of a lot bigger than the rest of us. By the time he finally ate it, some of the candy probably wasn't fit for human consumption but that didn't seem to bother him.

I remember pranks too, from simple to elaborate, and from benign to mildly destructive. If chickens knew what happened to their eggs on Halloween, they might reconsider being so diligent in producing them. I wonder still if my mother has ever figured out why we seemed to run out of toilet paper close to Halloween; she must have seen some of it hanging from trees and houses. Both my father and my father-in-law are of the World War II generation and have memories of Halloween way-back-then. They remember, if not the real thing, then at least stories about turning over outhouses at Halloween. Try to explain turning over an outhouse to one of today's kids who was raised in disposable diapers.

I am many times blessed to be the father of my great twelve year old son Jake. One of those blessings has been the fun of getting Jake dressed up and ready to go trick-or-treating and then making the trip with him. We started Jake early; he went trick-or-treating the first time at age seven months dressed as Rambo the Survivalist. At that age he had no idea what was going on but he seemed to enjoy it. The past couple of years I have been away from home on Halloween and couldn't go with Jake but I have managed to go to the home of friends to enjoy the evening watching their children or grandchildren.

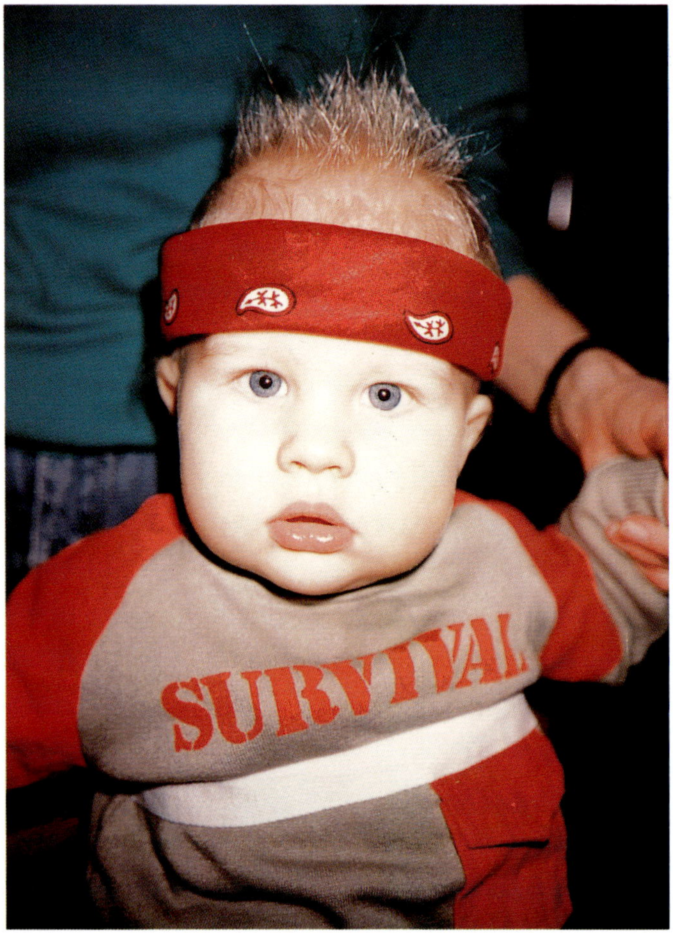

My son Jake at 7 months, dressed as "Rambo the Survivalist" on his first Halloween trick-or-treating expedition.

The perspective of Halloween from outside of the door asking for treats is different than the perspective you have from inside the door handing out the treats. Inside the door you are warm and cozy and you already know what you have for treats. Outside the door one is exposed to the elements, excited and delighted, or disappointed for that matter, when you see the treats. Also outside you must be ready at any moment to be scared. Still I prefer to be on the outside.

Tripping around the neighborhood you can see all the decorations people put out for Halloween. I'm glad to see that each year it seems there are more homes decorated and that the decorations are more elaborate. You should take the time at Halloween to go around your neighborhood, even if you only drive, and check out the decorations. Look at the elaborate jack-o'-lanterns, the lawn decorations, the window decorations, the spider webs, the gravestones, and the human-form dummies. Many homes have motorized displays and some even are sound enhanced. One particular setup I remember seeing a couple of years back involved a coffin in the front yard. It was motorized so the lid opened to reveal a corpse (also motorized) that actually sat up once the lid was open. People aren't doing all that work just "for the kids." Looking at all the effort put into Halloween you know there has got to be more to it—these people are having fun.

What didn't exist when I was a kid are the numerous and very elaborate "Haunted Houses" that now are set up for kids. I like these especially since they open up well before Halloween and thus help extend the holiday.

It is a fact that Halloween has become the second biggest holiday in the U.S. in terms of money spent; second only to Christmas. Of course much of this money is spent on things like buying or renting costumes, treats to hand out, parties, greeting cards, and the like but there is a big and growing market for Halloween decorations of all types. I have had some commercial Halloween designs in my resin-cast collection over the years. Although these items didn't do as well as the Christmas items, they certainly evoked a disproportionate number of comments from customers. People like to be amused and carving Halloween decorations can allow you to do some creative work that others will appreciate.

The problem with commercially produced Halloween decorations is that they are becoming "sanitized". By that I mean their design is being moved in a certain direction to avoid being "politically incorrect." One of the great things about being a kid at Halloween was being scared. Scary things are thrilling. Why do you suppose there are so many horror novels and movies? Because people, especially kids, love to be scared in a safe way.

Today you will find that commercial decorations have to be much more benign. Scary is out! "Cute" is much more acceptable in these designs now. "Whimsical" is thought to be better than scary or realistic. Witches can't be too scary—a happy witch is a good witch today. Devils and devilish images are definitely taboo if you are concerned with the reactions of some zealous religious groups. Of course these design influences don't have to affect you if you are carving things for yourself or as gifts but they are a consideration if you have any commercial intentions. That said, please remember that my designs are aimed at this commercial world.

Chapter Two
Everything You Needed To Know About Halloween

Once I started to create this book, I became interested in knowing more about Halloween. I did a little research and found out some interesting things about this holiday.

Halloween occurs at a unique time of the year. This time of year has historically, in our northern latitudes, been the time between fall and winter when all harvesting should have been completed and the fruits of the harvest stored away. Often this is the time of year when the first snowfall occurs. It can be viewed as the time between the light portion of the year and the dark; the time between the living part of the year and the dead part of the year. The season represents a definite turning point in the year.

There seems to be some consensus that our present day Halloween has roots in an ancient Druid festival that fell at this same time of year. Perhaps because of the symbology of this in-between time separating the living and the dead, the Druids believed that on the last night of October the spirits of the dead could roam the earth. Bonfires were built to keep the spirits away for the fear was that the spirits might decide to inhabit a living body.

The Celts also had similar beliefs and would dress up in costumes and hold noisy gatherings to make themselves and their homes less attractive to spirits. Some cultures actually believed that sleeping in a sitting position would help keep spirits from inhabiting the body of a sleeping person. This belief was based on the idea that spirits roaming in the night would confuse a fully reclining sleeper with a dead person and would feel free to take over that body

A European custom called "souling" is believed to be the source of our modern day custom of "trick-or-treating." Early Christians would go about the countryside visiting villages and homes begging for "soul cakes." The beggars would say prayers for the souls of dead relatives of those providing the "soul cakes." Part of the beliefs at that time were that the souls of the dead resided somewhere in "limbo" and prayers could help the soul move on to heaven.

Some of these customs were absorbed into Roman culture and from there adapted into modern culture over the intervening years. It is probable that the celebration of Halloween came here to us from Ireland with the Irish migrations of the mid-nineteenth century.

In the Catholic calendar November 1 is "All Saints' Day," also known as "All Hallows Day." This is the feast day on which the church celebrates its saints, martyrs, and others. Apparently early celebrations of this type were held at other times of the year; however, these became a three day feast ending on November 1, while the present day holiday of "All Saints' Day" is now a single Holy day. The juxtaposition of this feast with the earlier pagan autumn festivals of the spirits is probably not coincidental. Many Christian holidays were overlaid onto earlier celebrations existing in cultures that were undergoing conversion.

In the Catholic calendar November 2 is "All Souls' Day." This is a day to solicit, through prayer, mercy for souls other than those of the Saints. Once more the similarity among the older pagan customs regarding souls roaming the earth and the evolved Catholic practices regarding souls (spirits) shows itself. This time of year, after the harvest and before the bitterest part of the year, clearly was and is a time of the year for the spiritual population to reflect on life and death.

Knowing now that Halloween occurs the evening before "All Saints' Day," also known as "All Hallows Day," we can see how the evening before "All Hallows Day" has come, over the years, to be corrupted from "All Hallows Evening" into "Halloween." There you have it!

Chapter Three
Halloween Designs, Notes, and Patterns

The subjects available for Halloween carving designs may seem obvious, but let's review some of the general categories and what can be done with them.

Ghosts

Ghosts may be the most flexible of all subjects for Halloween designs since they are amorphous and may be standing, sitting, riding, popping out of things, or even flying. Ghosts can hold things and do things that add to the whimsy and impact of the overall designs. Ghosts look great in groups, especially if they are of different sizes. Ghosts can be playful, like my "I Love Treats" ghost.

"I Love Treats" Ghost. This piece is painted with acrylics and finished by antiquing. Wires hold up the sign.

The pattern for "The Ghost With The Most" shows that I played with many of the design elements for Halloween, combining them into one design. I might have overdone it here, since I was trying to exaggerate the point that elements should be combined. This ghost is wearing a witch's hat and holding a witch's black cat. The three jack-o`-lanterns include one with a baby ghost popping out of it. The tombstone is one of many possible tombstones that you can do.

The pattern for "Lon's Ghost" shows a fun combination of Halloween design elements. Lon's ghost is pointing at his tombstone while a black cat also points to it. A jack-o`-lantern sits atop the tombstone.

I have included a page of design notes to give you some pointers about ghosts. You can do fat ghosts, skinny ghosts, flying ghosts, and others—anything you can come up with. The ghosts I drew for you are pretty plain; you should add to them to get a more complete design. Note that you can make them happy, sad, mad, singing, as you wish pretty much just by modifying the mouth shape.

"I Love Treats" back view.

THE GHOST WITH THE MOST.

2" BASSWOOD

DRAWN ACTUAL SIZE

'98

LON'S GHOST

1" BASSWOOD

DRAWN ACTUAL SIZE

'98

Tombstone Humor

Tombstones and tombstone humor caught my fancy while I was working on this book. These subjects give you something quick and easy to carve but also something where you can really go out on a limb and show your creativity.

The tombstones I drew in my design notes are all pretty much straight up and down but you could easily make them more wacky shapes and probably add to the overall appeal. The tombstones are really only props for you to use in coming up with things to add to the composition that will be humorous. Thinking up names was fun for us ... my son included. I have seen many different names on these humorous tombstones over the years but I think we still came up with a couple of our own. Give it a try.

Ghosts in the tombstones should be positioned in whimsical ways like the ones I drew. Placing them standing, sitting, leaning, or whatever will add to the whimsy of the design. Add other elements to make an appealing composition and then give it a try.

Witches

Witches are great subjects for Halloween carvings. One of my witches is the "Wacky Witch of the West" equipped with six guns, boots, bandanna, and big belt buckle. Another one is the "Halloween Sandwich" which is a play on words taking its inspiration from the sign board sandwich.

Right: "Halloween Sandwich." This piece is based on the word play with the sandwich board.

"Wacky Witch of the West". She has cowboy boots, a huge championship size belt buckle, six guns, bandanna, and a cowboy hat.

"Wacky Witch of the West" back view.

"Halloween Sandwich" back view.

There can be general purpose witches and special purpose witches—like kitchen witches or garden witches. I first became aware of kitchen witches several years ago and, although I haven't seen any lately, I think they are still something that would be fun to carve. The kitchen witches I am most familiar with were riding their brooms. Each came equipped with a string so they could hang somewhere in the kitchen or in a kitchen window from which they could presumably preside over all the goings-on in the kitchen. I guess a little magic wouldn't hurt the recipes of some cooks.

Garden witches are similar in that they have elements of design that relate specifically to gardening. A garden witch that could be placed with an indoor plant or indoor garden would be a fun carving. If there are kitchen witches and garden witches then why not others? Do you know someone who enjoys quilting, sewing, music, or art? How about a witch based on one of these themes as a great carved gift?

Common elements in witch designs are the hat, the boots, possibly a cat, or possibly a broom. Witches don't have to have green faces and clothing colors other than straight black are O.K. too. Uncommon witch designs could include things like a witch on a motorcycle, an airplane or hang glider, or with animals other than cats as familiars—how about lizards or pigs?

There are several pages of design ideas I drew up for the book. Review these design ideas and notes to help you come up with your own designs. The hat is a critical part of a witch design and hats can be many shapes. The straight old hat still works but bending, twisting, or elongating the hat adds interest. The hat can be used to show motion as if it were being bent back by the wind. Symbols can be added to the hat to emphasize the mystical or the whimsical.

A witch design can easily be done where the cloak or coat droops all the way to the base but if the boots do show in the carving they become important. There are probably an infinite number of boot styles from basic to absurd.

Add things to the design for your witch. Put symbols on the coat, particularly if you do a special purpose witch. Put pockets on the coat and designs on the pocket or have things hanging out of the pockets. Give her a necklace, or a magic wand, or a great broom. Here is where you can have fun.

One challenge on the witch design will be the face. Unless you are a skilled carver I suggest you stick with the simplest face; the one I call "Nothing But Nose." In this design you need only carve a nose and leave the remainder of the face rounded but not detailed. You can then draw a simple face on and paint over it. The sides of the face are dictated by the shape of the hair - look at the basic shape I used in the design notes and see that it emphasizes the cheeks and chin of the witch.

If you are more skilled, you can detail the face. Add an especially long and bumpy nose. Detail the eyes and don't forget things like the exaggerated chin and the warts.

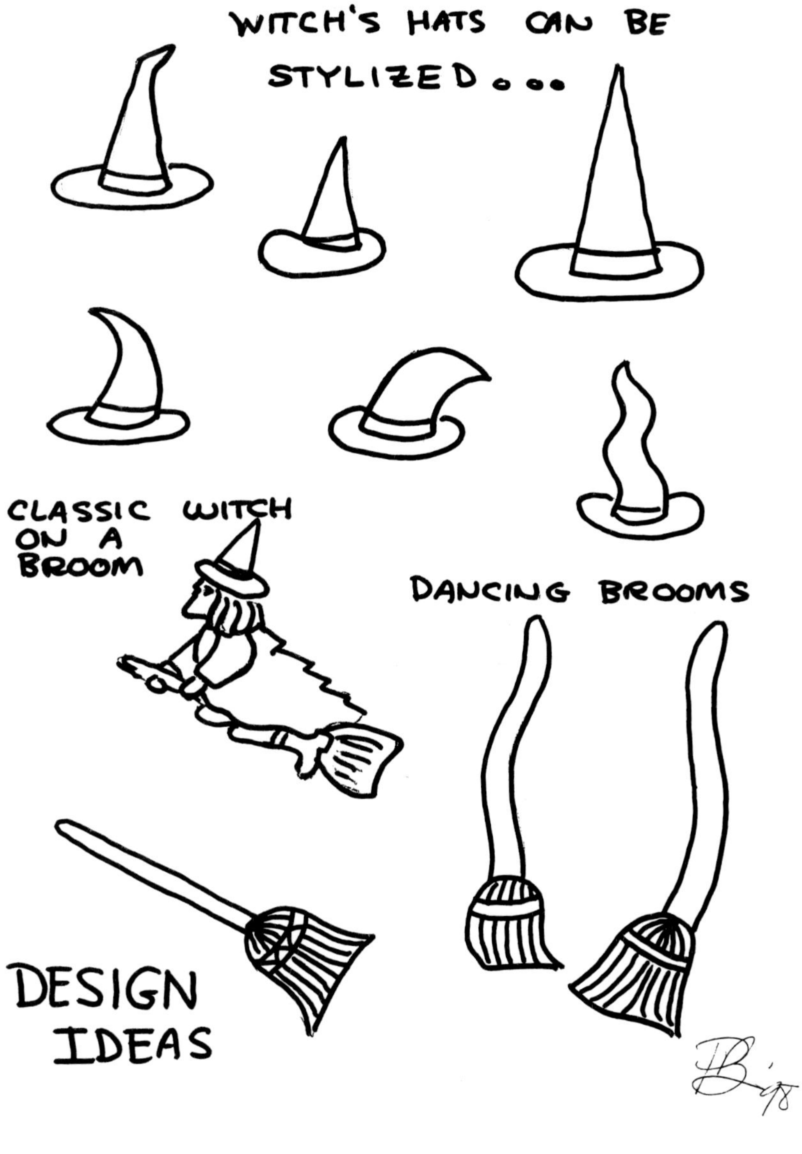

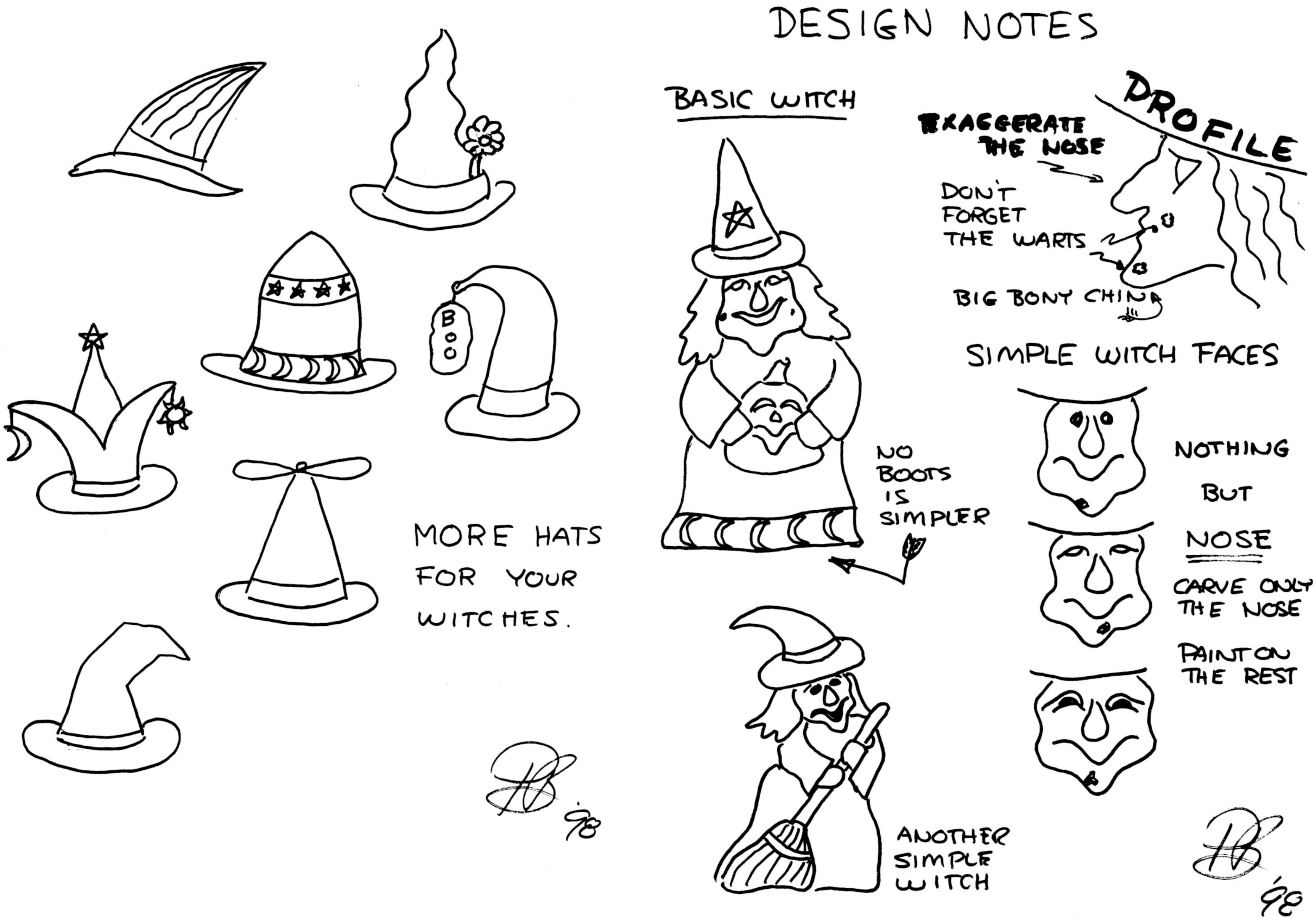
DESIGN NOTES
MORE HATS
FOR YOUR
WITCHES.
'98
BASIC WITCH
NO
BOOTS
IS
SIMPLER
ANOTHER
SIMPLE
WITCH
PROFILE
EXAGGERATE
THE NOSE
DON'T
FORGET
THE WARTS
BIG BONY CHIN
SIMPLE WITCH FACES
NOTHING
BUT
NOSE
CARVE ONLY
THE NOSE
PAINT ON
THE REST
'98

WITCH'S GEAR

SYMBOLS ON THE HAT?

WHAT ABOUT A PATCHWORK WITCH?

IF WITCHES HAD POCKETS - WHAT WOULD YOU FIND INSIDE AND OUTSIDE?

SYMBOLS ON COAT OR CLOAK...

DESIGN IDEAS

'98

Pumpkins

Pumpkin designs are somewhat limited by the general requirement that they be recognized as pumpkins or jack-o'-lanterns but they can still be fun and whimsical. One of my first Halloween carvings was "Mr. Pumpkinhead Goes Trick or Treating," in which a figure with a carved pumpkin head wore a mask to try and disguise the fact that he was a pumpkin.

Pumpkins with people-like features can be fun. I have done several of these including the pumpkin brothers: "Pumpkin Grumpkin" and "Pumpkin Plumpkin." Grumpkin was having a bad mood day while Plumpkin's problem involved an obviously upset stomach. These two brothers were carved as they appeared just before they were arrested for fertilizer theft—a federal crime in which they stole fertilizer right out of the ground in broad daylight.

"Mr. Pumpkinhead Goes Trick or Treating."

"Pumpkin Grumpkin."

"Mr. Pumpkinhead" back view.

"Pumpkin Grumpkin" back view.

Others among my people pumpkin designs were "Erik the Orange"—a Viking Pumpkin—and "Albert Einpunkin," recognizable by his shaggy gray hair (a cut up old gray T-shirt). For quite some time I had a block against adding other materials to my carvings. I think this came about from the belief that, as a woodcarver, everything I created should be carved out of a single piece of wood. That concept is nonsense when working on whimsical designs. Adding non-wood items to your creations can add a dimension not otherwise found. Look around at whimsical works and you will see that many have multiple materials that show different textures and qualities.

"Pumpkin Plumpkin."

"Erik the Orange" a Viking pumpkin.

"Pumpkin Plumpkin" back view.

"Erik the Orange" back view.

Another of my carvings, "Pumpkins 'R' Us", uses non-wood elements. There is a bale of straw on the ground and some raffia pumpkins piled up. These added elements give an extra touch to the piece that would have been tough to do in wood.

"Albert Einpunkin" the great pumpkin genius. Note the gray hair painted under the gray cloth strips.

"Albert Einpunkin" back view.

"Pumpkins 'R' Us". Note how the raffia pumpkins add to the texture.

"Pumpkins 'R' Us" back view. Note the bale of hay and hay spread on the ground.

My carving "Dr. Punkinstein" combines pumpkins with the movie themes of Halloween. I tried to get the doctor to look as much like the Frankenstein monster as possible by using scars and the metal shafts sticking out of his neck. Extra humor is added with all the implements he uses in his "plastic surgery while you wait" business. Painted on the sides of the box are "Doc in the Box" and "Hours - sunset to sunrise." If you turned the box around you would see that it is an outhouse.

"Dr. Punkinstein". Note the figurine stands in the box or outside.

Jack-o'-lanterns are great subjects for pumpkin carving. Stylized jack-o'-lanterns are quite appealing as are elaborately carved ones. Groups make good subjects and should be of different sizes and could have exaggerated shapes. A carved jack-o'-lantern turned into a candle holder would make a great Halloween creation.

A page of design notes is provided to stimulate your thinking about jack-o'-lantern designs. Give your creations shape—remember some real pumpkins you have seen. Lean your pumpkin into or away from some other element in the design to emphasize it. Play with the eyes and the mouth. Put pupils into the eyes and use them to highlight something else in the design; whatever the pumpkin looks at will automatically draw the eyes of the viewer. Go for lots of teeth or just a few teeth or even just one tooth. Happy mouths are cute but you can do "down at the corners" unhappy or mad pumpkins too if they fit into your design.

"Dr. Punkinstein" back view.

PUMPKINS CAN COME IN MANY SHAPES....

CROOKED IS CUTE!

PUT PUPILS IN WHACKY SPOTS FOR WHIMSICAL PUMPKINS.

TRY DIFFERENT SHAPES FOR EYES.

AN ORTHODONTIST'S DREAM!

MOST JACK-O'-LANTERNS TODAY ARE SMILING - BUT THEY STILL CAN HAVE SNAGGLED TEETH.

DESIGN NOTES

'98

Movie Creatures

Movies are a great source of inspiration for Halloween carvings. Frankenstein would make a great carving. I have done a takeoff on the Mummy with my "Mummy's Herbal Body Wrap". Count Dracula was the obvious inspiration for "Dracula's Bloodbank - Give `till It Hurts". A Werewolf would make a great carving, particularly if he was worked into a more whimsical carving. The Grim Reaper, the Headless Horseman, the Hunchback, even the Bride of Frankenstein are other potential subjects for you to consider.

"Mummy's Egyptian Herbal Body Wrap".

"Mummy's" back view.

"Dracula's Blood Bank".

There is a pattern provided for "Mummy's Egyptian Herbal Body Wrap". This is a pretty simple carving but quite pleasing when finished. I chose to have the mummy holding an advertising sign but you could easily modify the design as you wish.

In this design I exposed only a little of the mummy's face but there could be interesting things done with exposing more of the mummy. I kept all the wrappings tight but they could just as easily be shown loose and falling off. Mummies are generally linked with Egypt; perhaps you can work some other Egyptian design elements into a mummy carving.

A pattern for "Count Dracula's Bloodbank" is provided for you. This design emphasizes the humor of the vampire/blood connection but many other variations are possible. The key element in a Dracula design is the recognizability of the design; it must look like Dracula ... or at least like a vampire. The "fangs," the hairline, the red lips, and the clothing are all elements that help define the vampire. Try this design or think up one of your own and give it a shot—it's fun.

THE MUMMY

(REVERSE)

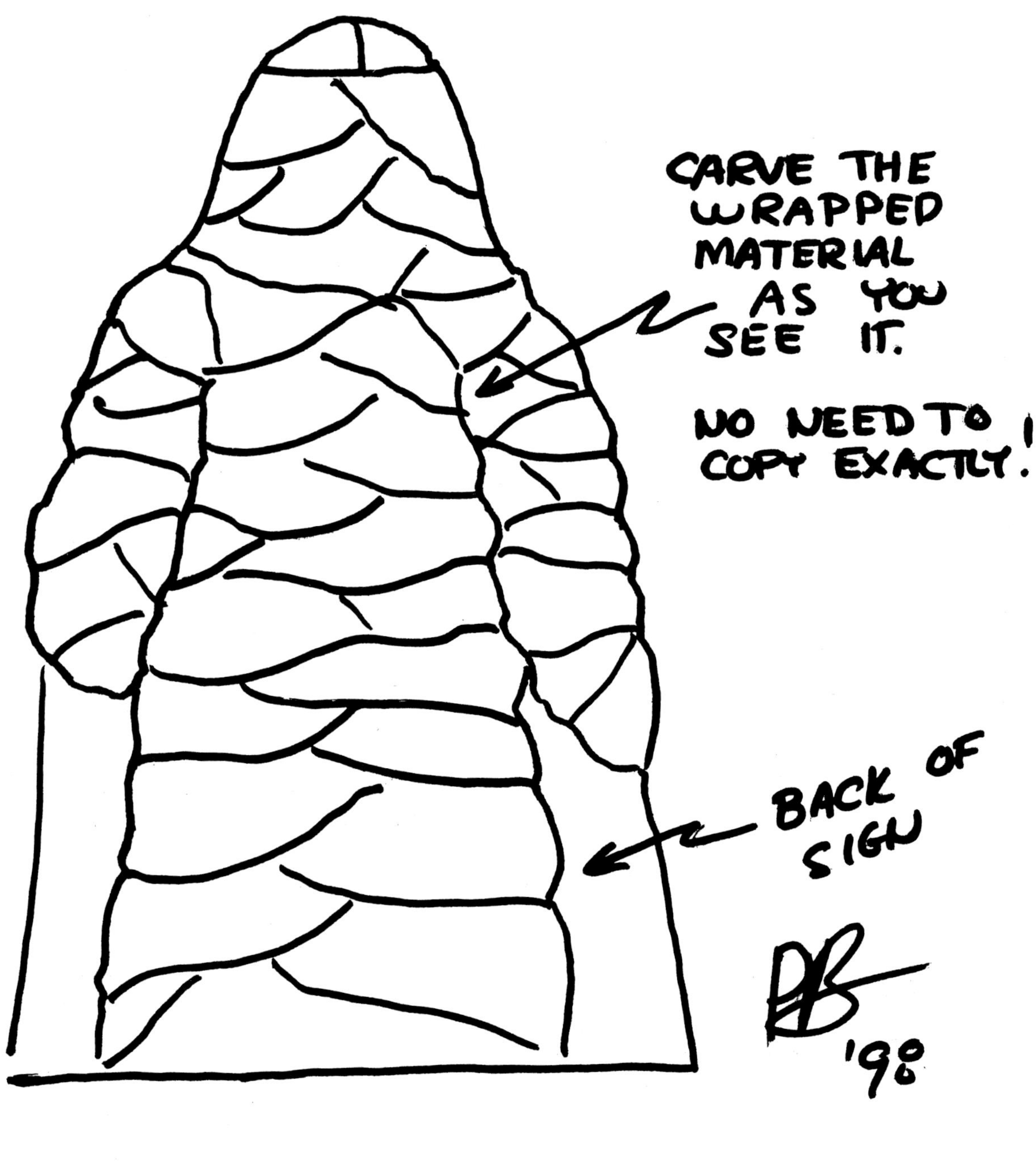

THE MUMMY

• CARVED FROM 3" x 4" BASSWOOD
• ACRYLIC PAINT

BLOODSHOT EYE

EXPOSE AS MUCH OF FACE AS YOU LIKE

NOSE SHOWS PARTIALLY - COULD CARVE WITH WHOLE NOSE SHOWING

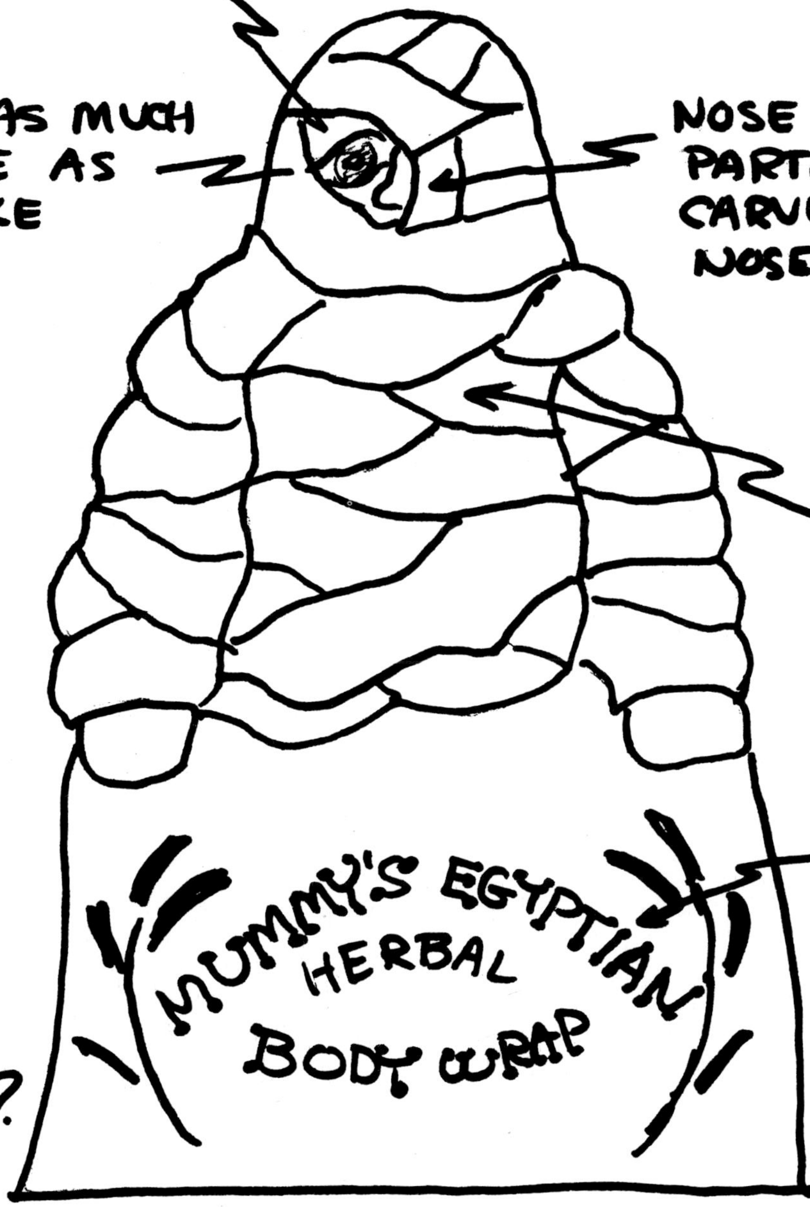

A LITTLE HEART WOULD BE CUTE ♡

PUT ANY CUTE PHRASE YOU WANT HERE

HOW ABOUT A CAMEL?

OR A PYRAMID?

OR HEIROGLYPHICS?

DRAWN ACTUAL SIZE

ABOUT 6" TALL

'90

COUNT DRACULA

COUNT DRACULA

(REVERSE)

'98

Cats, Bats, and Other Animals

Nothing is more traditional to Halloween than the black cat. Cats can be done in many shapes and positions. Cats work well when combined with other design themes like pumpkins, ghosts, witches of course, and others. Bats are great animal themes too. Bats can hang from things upside down or perch upon things. Bats can be shown with wings spread or folded. Rats, snakes, and of course spiders can be added to carvings to help enhance the "creepy" aspects of the carving.

A page of design notes is provided to show you some bat and cat shapes. Halloween black cats are generally shown with their backs arched but they don't have to be. Bats and cats can be very stylized designs as long as the shape in general suggests "bat" or "cat."

Halloween Signs

I like to carve signs and have had some fun with Halloween signs. In one large sign I combined many of the design elements for Halloween—like bats, cats, brooms, etc.—into letters spelling out Halloween. Some of my other signs are "I Love Jack-O`-Lanterns", "Halloween is a Treat", "Boo To You Too", "No Tricks", "7 Pumpkins", and even one very esoteric rendition of "Pumpkin Pi" (the mathematical symbol Pi made from pumpkins).

"No Tricks" sign.

"Halloween Is a Treat" sign.

"Boo to You Too" sign.

"I Love Jack-O'-Lanterns" sign.

"7 Pumpkins" sign.

"I Love Halloween" sign. Note that the word Halloween is spelled by using symbols from the season in place of letters: a bat for the letter "H", a hat for the letter "A", and so on.

"Pumpkin Pi" sign.

The pattern for my "No Tricks" sign is provided. Sign carving is straight forward once you have designed the piece and done a drawing for layout. The fun for me here was to come up with the ideas. Let's see what you can do.

NO TRICKS

1" THICK
BASSWOOD

I PUT TOOL MARKS ON
BACKGROUND
FOR CONTRAST.

DRAWN ACTUAL SIZE

ABOUT 7" TALL

DB '98

Other Halloween Things

There are many other possible items for Halloween designs including: skeletons, coffins, corpses, goblins, ghouls, and maybe even trolls.

Blending a Design

A key to Halloween design is the blending of elements into a single design. Simple groupings of similar design elements works well with Halloween designs. Groups of jack-o'-lanterns and ghosts are particularly cute but groups of witches, skeletons, movie figures, and other items can be great. Mixing of elements works well too and gives more whimsy to designs. From the simplest element swappings (such as putting a witch's hat on a pumpkin or a ghost) to more elaborate mixings, this technique will help you move to a more whimsical design.

That is the end of the discussion on design. Now it is time to try some carvings.

Chapter Four
Carving The Ghost With the Most

This carving was made from a 2" block of basswood. There isn't a lot of depth to this piece, which makes it highly suitable for beginning carvers.

The tools used on this project are some basic gouges ("U" and "V"), a micro gouge, and a knife. I also use a Foredom rotary power grinder to clean up my design after I have carved it with the hand tools. The entire project can easily be accomplished with a knife and sandpaper if you wish.

I use a carver's arm to hold my workpiece. The workpiece is secured to the carver's arm with a carver's screw. The screw penetrates the bottom of the workpiece, holding the carving tight. Of course, any hold down technique will work as long as you can reach the necessary areas of the piece. You may actually wish to hold the piece in your hand. That will work, but please be careful.

Begin by transferring the pattern to a block of wood and then sawing the pattern out of the block. Follow the instructions that accompany the photos. Good luck.

This is the cut-out for "The Ghost With The Most". The pattern was transferred using carbon paper and then the piece was sawn from 2" thick basswood.

Using a large, shallow gouge or a knife, start by carving back the top of the hat so it will lean backward.

Make a stop cut along the brim of the hat and remove the wood below the cut. Stop cuts may be made with a straight gouge or a knife.

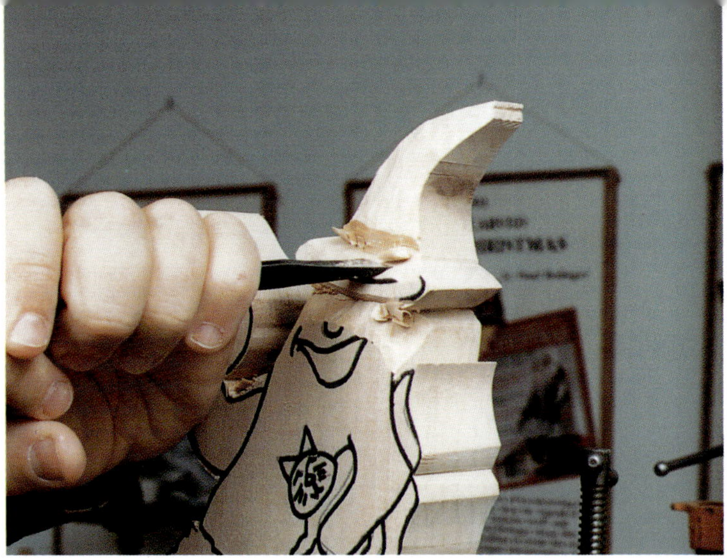

Use a gouge to cut up under the hat brim at the top of the ghost's face and also to shape the brim of the hat back some. Note that the process of carving will be like peeling an onion—we will go layer by layer. Do not try to take off too much wood at any time since you will be back over the piece several times. In this way you will keep the piece in balance as you go.

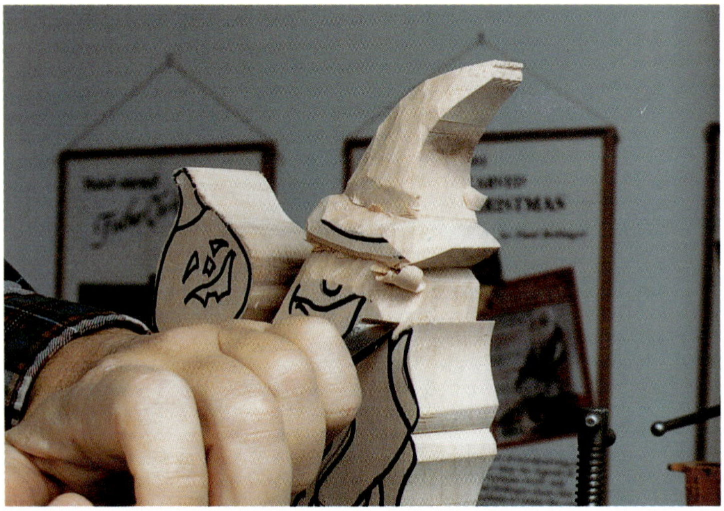

Use a gouge to round off the edges of the ghost's head.

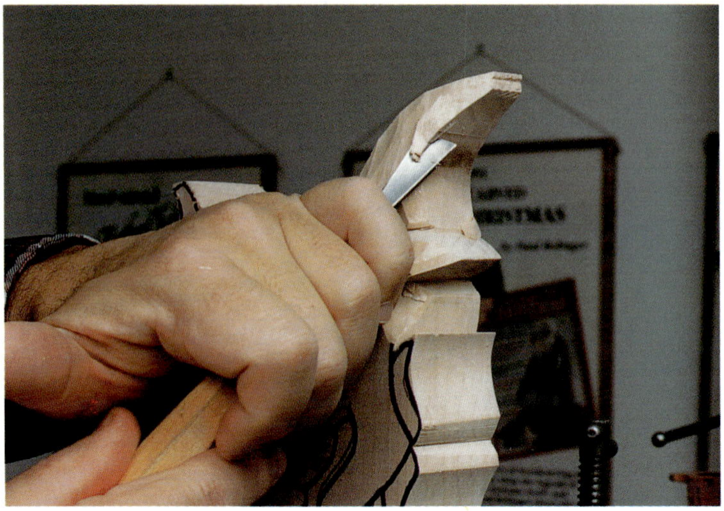

Push the hat back farther and round the edges.

Round the pumpkin in the ghost's hand.

Make a stop cut at the bottom of the pumpkin.

Remove wood from the ghost's arm below the pumpkin.

Use a "V" gouge to cut a groove separating the ghost's arm from his body along the pattern line. A knife would work well too.

Remove more wood from the arm and round the arm some. Remember not to go too far at any one time—just peel a layer from the onion.

Shape the pumpkin more. You will have to re-draw the pattern later.

Shape the face more. You will have to re-draw the pattern later.

Use a "V" gouge to cut a groove separating the cat's tail from the Ghost. Shape the body away from the tail.

Re-cut the stop cut along the bottom of the hat. Shape the top of the face back more by removing the wood up to the stop cut.

Shape the cat's tail back.

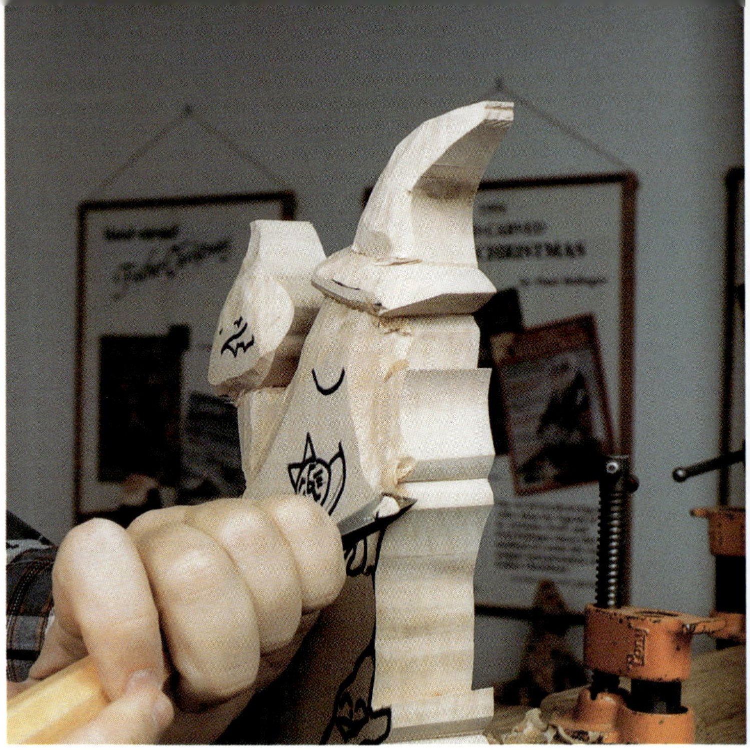

Push the tail back farther. Note that the tail I ended up carving does not match the pattern exactly. On the pattern, the tail looks like it wraps up and around the arm. Once I got into carving, the tail seemed to be better if it went under the arm and popped out at the top. Such slight differences will happen to you when you go from a 2D pattern to a 3D carving. It is part of the creative process.

Use a "V" gouge to define the back of the tail.

Remove the waste wood from behind the tail.

The wood in front, below, and behind the tail has been removed leaving the tail sticking up from the inside crook of the ghost's arm.

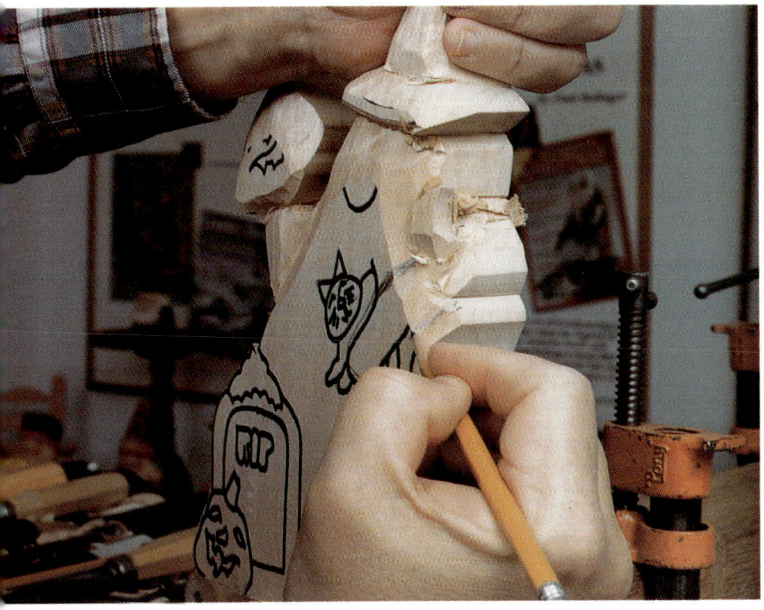

Mark the lines where the arm will be cut.

Cut along the upper and lower lines. Shape below the arm but leave enough wood for the cat's rump and legs.

Use a shallow "U" gouge to put a stop cut all around the outline of the cat's face and ears.

Remove wood from around the cat's head and ears.

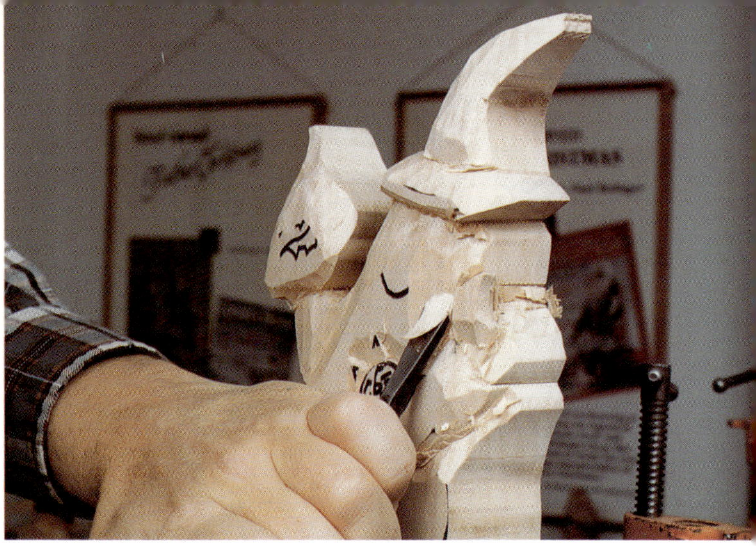

Remove more of the ghost's face area leaving the cat's tail alone so it separates more from the ghost.

Outline the cat's front legs and paws.

Remove more wood from the arm and shoulder behind the cat's tail. Leave the tail alone and be very careful not to remove the tail by accident.

Shape the wood below the ghost's arm back farther. You will have to re-draw the cat's rump and back legs later.

Cut farther into the ghost around the crook of the elbow to reveal more of the cat's tail.

Re-draw the cat's back legs. Note that the arm is beginning to wrap around the tail.

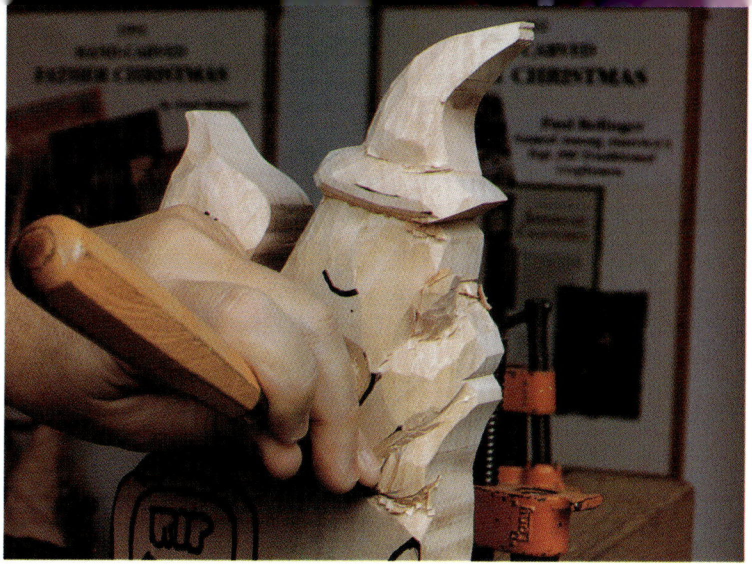

Continue to deepen the stop cuts around the feet and peel away the excess wood around the feet.

Use a gouge to outline the hind legs and make a stop cut below the feet.

Draw in the line showing the back of the hind leg. Leave plenty of wood to work on the legs later.

Outline the hind legs. Note that the wood has been cut away below the back feet.

Put stop cuts along the drawn line and begin to remove the wood from outside the line. This will leave the area for the hind legs.

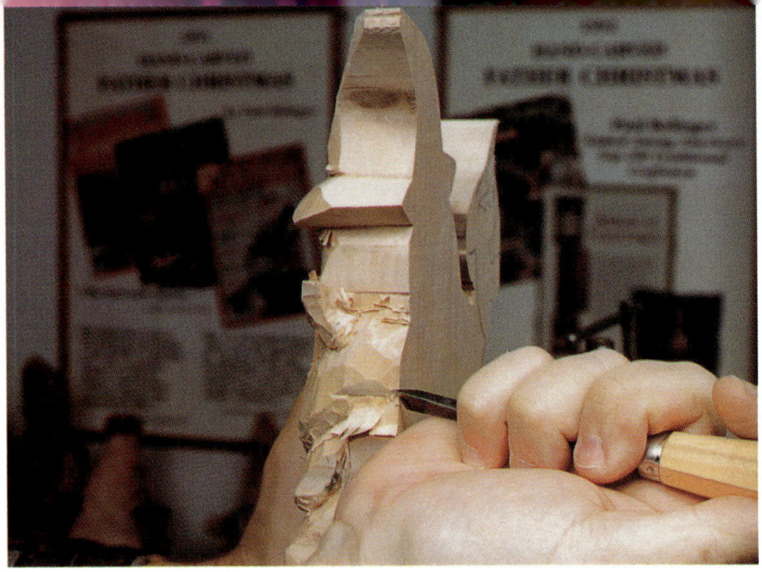

Remove waste wood from behind the legs.

Use a gouge to outline the baby ghost and pumpkin.

Remove more wood from the top of the ghost's arm and shape it back to the shoulder. Be careful not to damage the tail of the cat.

Remove the wood from the big ghost around the baby ghost and the pumpkin.

Now you can see the ghost's arm, the tail above the arm, and the hind feet of the cat below the arm.

Make stop cuts separating the baby from his pumpkin.

Remove some of the pumpkin and some of the baby ghost's arm to begin shaping them.

Draw in the lines for the side of the pumpkin and the baby ghost's left arm.

Remove waste wood from behind the baby ghost's arm and shape the side of the pumpkin.

Remove the waste wood at the back of the pumpkin.

Outline the pumpkin stem and lid that "popped off" the pumpkin to allow the baby ghost to emerge.

Shape the baby ghost's head back from his eyes up.

Begin to outline the pumpkin in front of the tombstone.

Outline the whole pumpkin and remove wood from tombstone around the pumpkin.

Outline the bat decoration at the top of the tombstone as well as the rest of the tombstone.

Remove the wood from around the raised edge of the tombstone.

Put a stop cut at the bottom of the tombstone.

Begin to remove the waste wood inside the tombstone.

Outline the "RIP" on the face of the tombstone.

Remove the wood from the face of the tombstone around the "RIP".

Outline the bat decoration at the top of the tombstone.

Use a small "U" gouge to outline the bat.

Remove the wood around the bat decoration. Note that the tombstone will not end up facing directly forward. The tombstone will be facing slightly to the left.

Separate and shape the stem and top of the pumpkin.

Draw the lines locating the side of the tombstone, the pumpkin, and the bat decoration. Use a "V" gouge or knife to outline these. Note how the left side of the tombstone is beginning to move back to the left.

Remove the waste wood behind the pumpkin, tombstone, and bat decoration.

Outline the head of the bat decoration.

Lightly carve away the bat body from the head.

The initial outlining and shaping of each component is now complete. Now you will begin the second pass around the figure giving it more shape and detail.

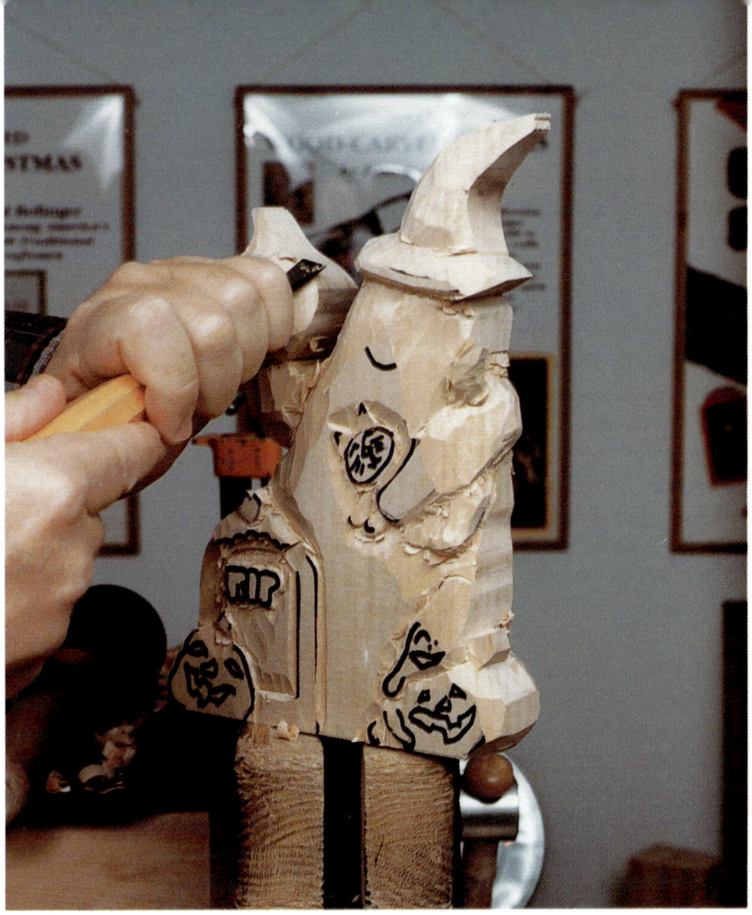

Go back and put more shape onto the upraised pumpkin.

Shape the ghost some more.

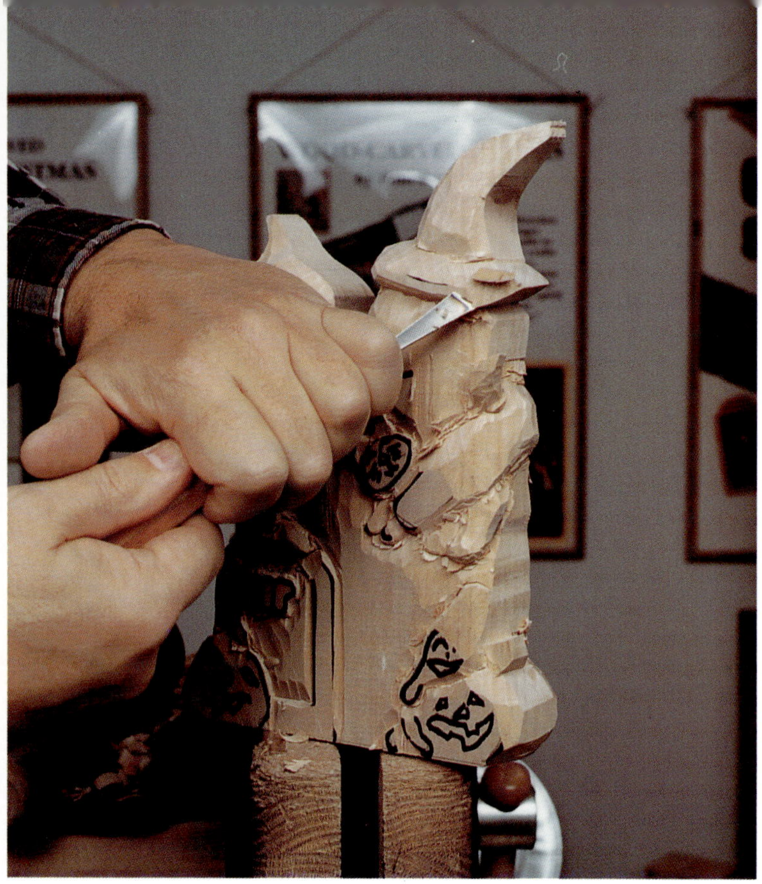

Shape the hat and brim more.

I used a small shallow "U" gouge to outline the facial features and cut them into the ghost. A knife would also work well.

Re-draw the ghost's face. I located the face based on the centerline of the piece plus the remainder of the lower lip left from the original pattern.

Outline the nose and cut away from around the nose. The ghost's nose will stick out from the face—not recede into it. Use a small gouge and continue to cut the facial features—go as deep as you like. These eyes are simple recesses below the brow. Painting will make up for the lack of carved detail.

Here you can see the facial features with eyes cut in, mouth cut in, and the nose left protruding.

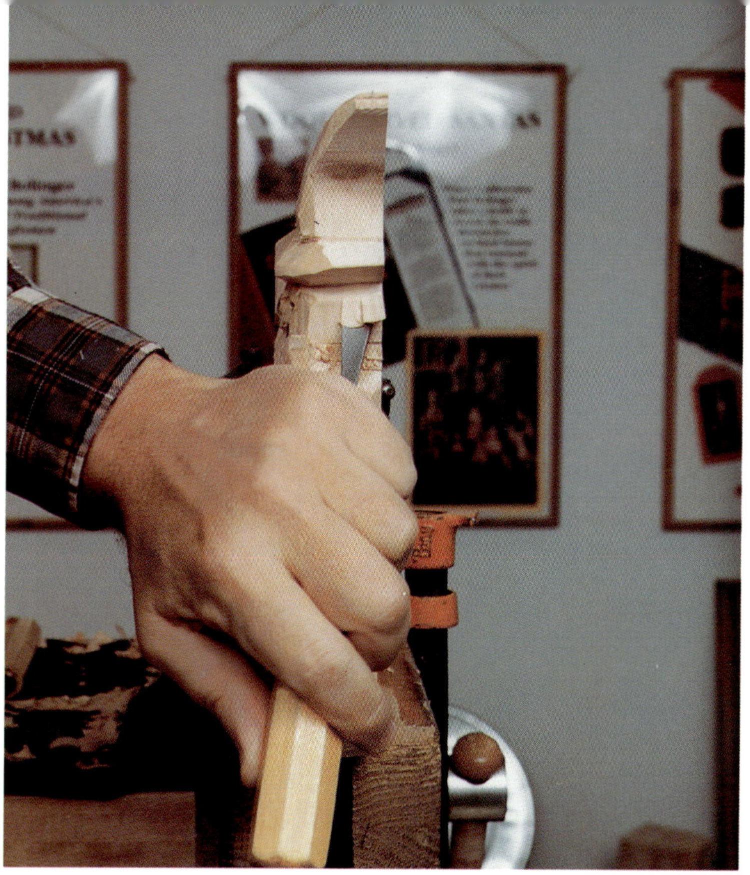

Now that the face is roughed out, go back to shaping the rest of the head.

I cut the mouth so it is open a little farther. This is a matter of taste.

Shape the hat.

Shape the bat decoration back on the left side to match the tombstone.

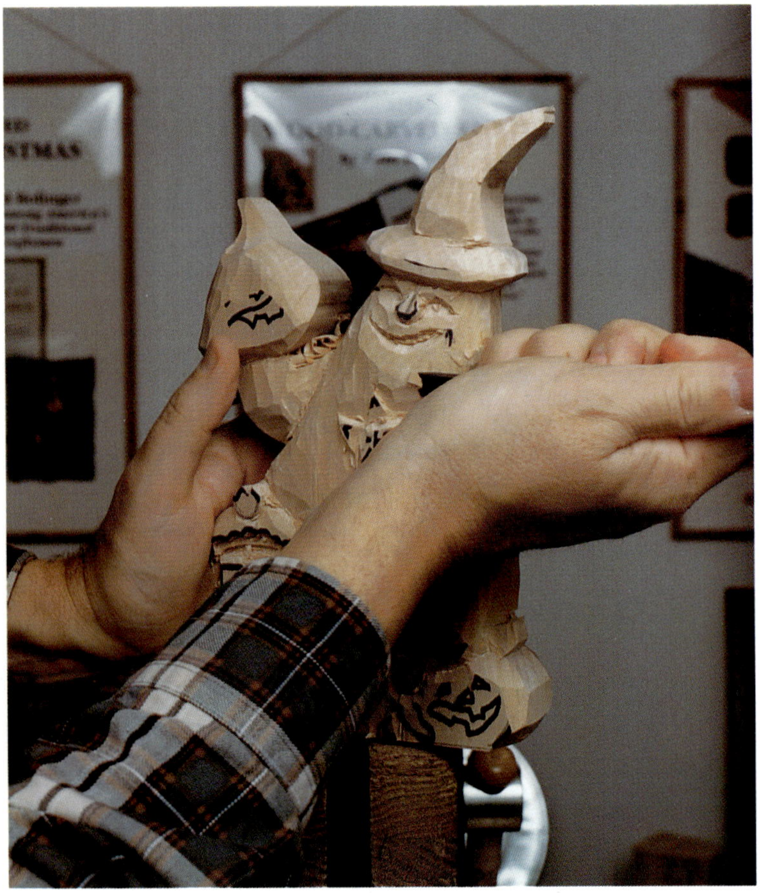

Round the body of the ghost to a shape that pleases you.

Shape the tombstone back on the left until you are happy with the look.

Cut away the face of the tombstone to match the leftward angle of the tombstone.

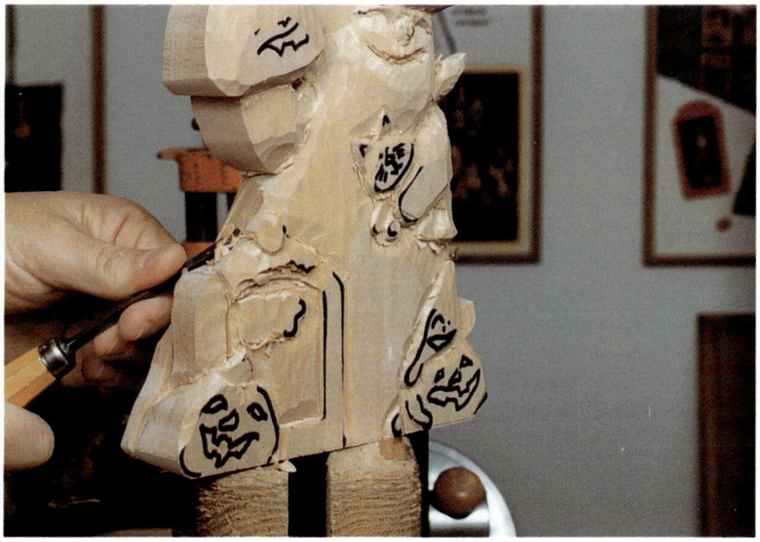

Remove more wood from the ghost behind the tombstone—go as far as you wish.

Outline the letters in the "RIP". I used a knife for this.

Shape the pumpkin.

Shape around the cat's hind feet and define them more.

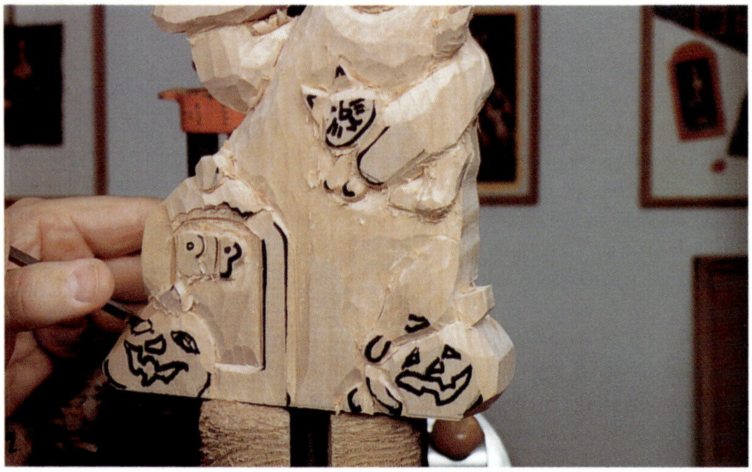

Cut the face into the pumpkin using a small gouge. Don't go too deep.

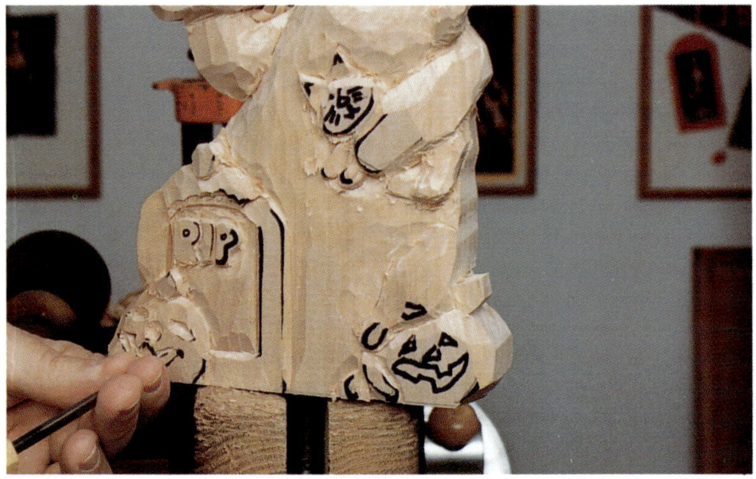

Cut the mouth into the pumpkin with a small U gouge.

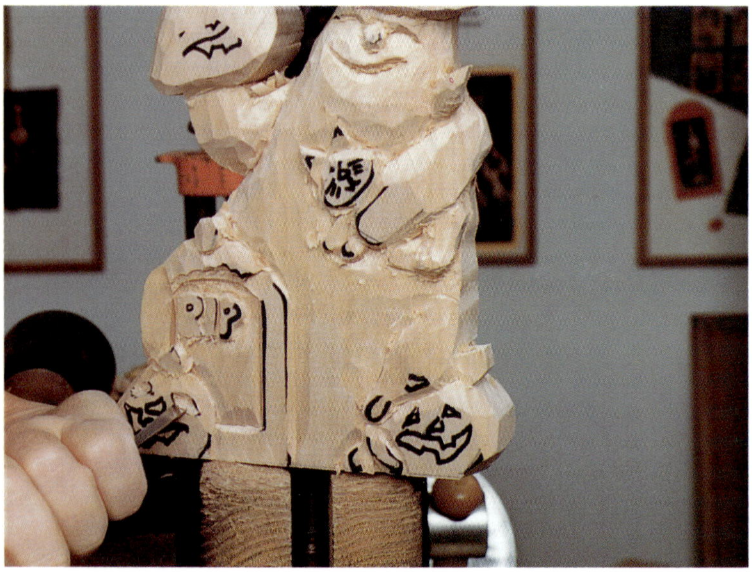

Shape the facial features as you wish.

Cut the face into the baby ghost. I used a micro "V" gouge to do this since the face was so small. A knife would work too.

Shape the cheeks of the pumpkin. If you cut the mouth off the left side, just re-draw it.

Cut the face into the pumpkin. I used a micro "V" gouge for this too.

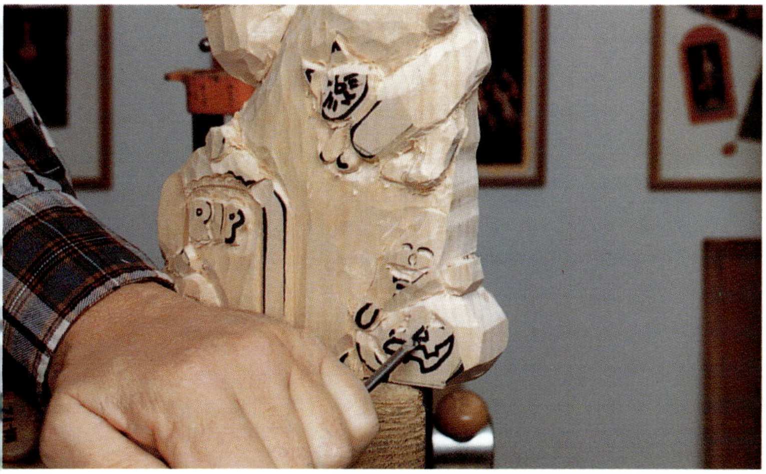

Use a shallow "U" gouge to cut in the pumpkin nose and mouth.

Shape the pumpkin so it looks somewhat to the right.

Outline the mouth and cut it into the pumpkin.

Re-draw the pumpkin face.

Cut the mouth in as deep as you wish.

Here I used a knife to outline the mouth. A gouge would work too.

Cut the mouth in with a small gouge.

Cut around the base of the pumpkin stem.

Cut in the nose.

Shape the stem.

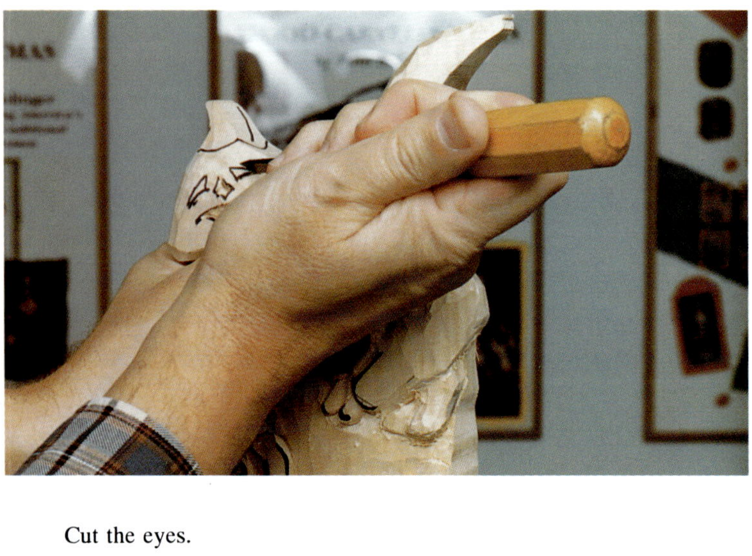

Cut the eyes.

Draw a line defining the back of the pumpkin stem. Remove the waste wood behind the stem.

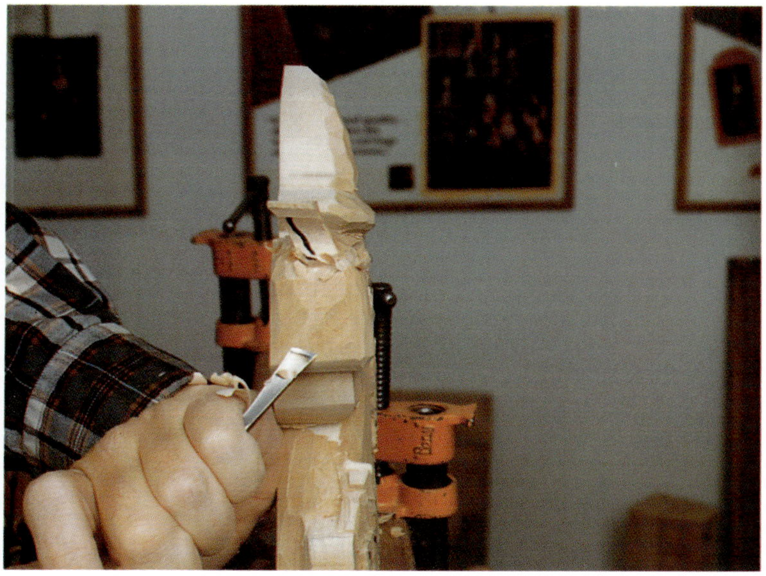

Shape the back of the pumpkin.

Draw a pattern on the back of the piece. Define the hat brim, the left shoulder, and the separation of the right arm from the body. Note: Ignore the lighter lines in the photo; they are from another, earlier project.

Shape the back of the hat. Use stop cuts along the lines at the bottom of the hat and cut up to the bottom.

Cut along the line behind the right arm. Shape the body and the arm lightly.

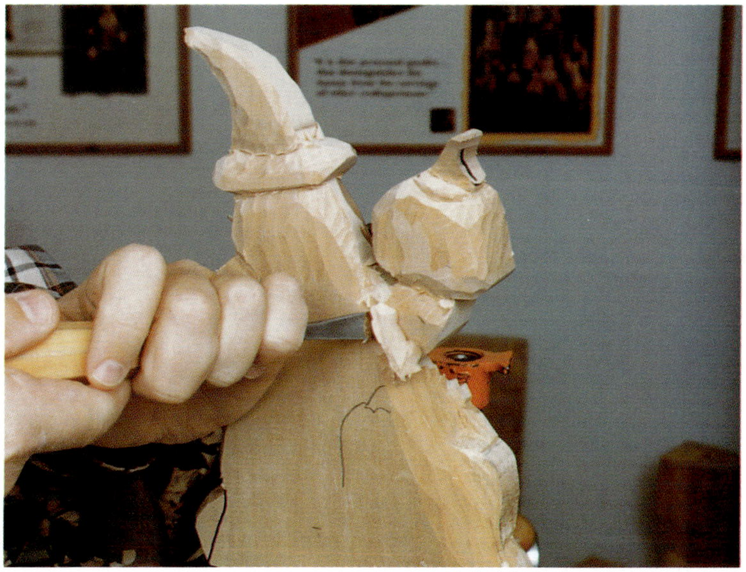

Shape the body and the arm.

Shape the left side of the back slightly.

Draw the line marking the top of the hat band. Outline the band.

Final shape the arms and upper body as you wish.

This is the final shape of the hat.

Outline the back of the baby ghost. Cut away the waste wood behind the baby.

This is the condition of the figure at the point where I stopped carving and moved on to the finish work. Note that I did not carve the cat's face at all; I left it for my wife to paint as she saw it.

Right side.

Left side.

Left front.

This is the sanded and base-coated figure. I used a Foredom flexible shaft rotary power tool with diamond burrs to clean out the crevices and rough areas of the carving. I then hand sanded lightly to prepare the wood for painting. You can clean up the carving with a knife and sandpaper if you wish.

Back view.

Right front view of the sanded figure.

Left front view.

Chapter Five
Carving Lon's Ghost

This project was produced from 1" basswood. The pattern was transferred to the wood with carbon paper and then sawn out of the wood. There is minimal carving in this project. Once the pattern is sawn out, the carving work amounts to little more than rounding the edges and highlighting the "breakpoints" between various elements of the design.

While I used some gouges for this project, it was completed mostly with a knife. After carving, the piece was cleaned up with a Foredom rotary tool and then hand sanded. You can easily complete the entire project with just a knife and some sandpaper.

I held this project in my hand for the entire time. With 1" wood there is often not enough room to use a carver's screw on the bottom of the piece and the work is often so small that the hold-down mechanism gets in the way. Go ahead and hold the piece but please be careful.

Follow the instructions that accompany the photos and good luck.

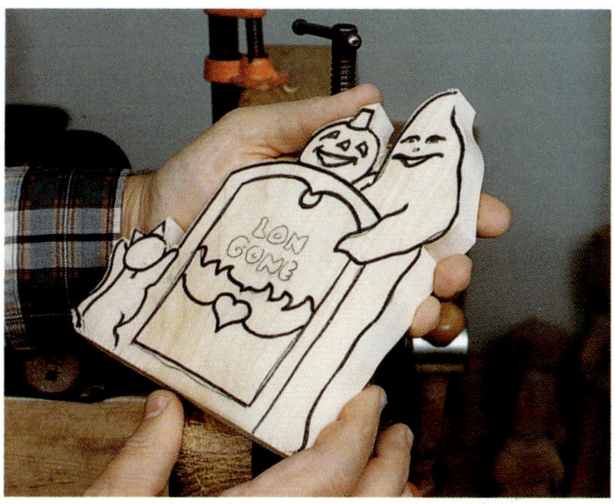

This is the front view of Lon's Ghost once it has been sawn out of 1" basswood. The pattern was transferred using carbon paper.

Back view. You may wish to omit carving the back and just paint it solid black to save time.

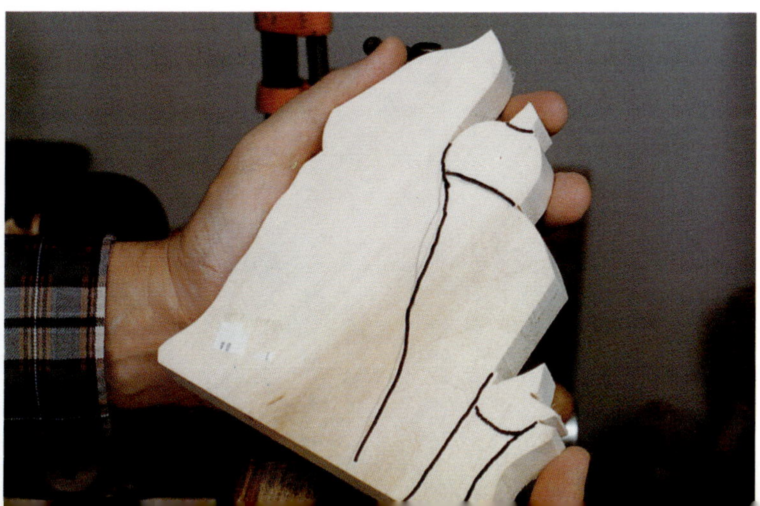

Here I used a knife to outline the tombstone.

Continue using the knife to outline the arm.

Remove the wood from the ghost, shaping the spook as you go.

Here I used a knife to shape the ghost.

Shaping the ghost.

Outline the top of the arm.

Outline the hand and the pointing finger.

Outline the inside of the tombstone.

Remove the waste wood along the areas you outlined.

Outline the left side of the ghost.

Shape the right side of the ghost.

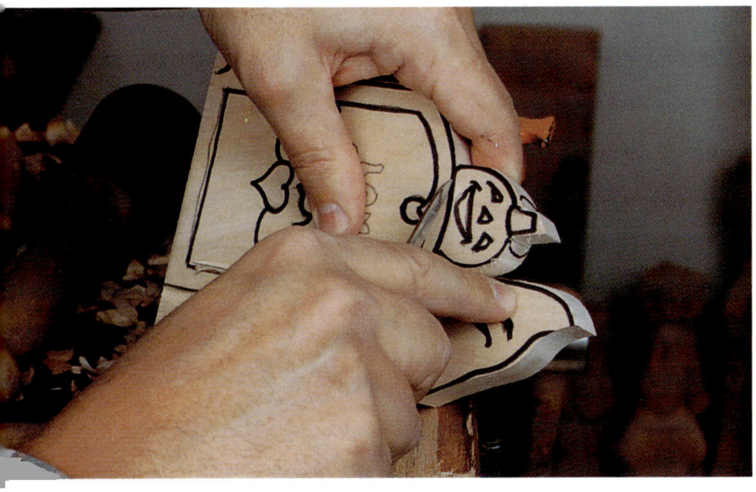

Outline the top of the tombstone.

Shape the left side of the ghost.

Remove the wood above the tombstone where you have outlined it.

Make a stop cut along the bottom of the tombstone.

Remove the wood from the face of the tombstone.

Outline the left side of the tombstone.

Outline the inside top of the tombstone.

Outline the bottom of the design on the tombstone using a medium shallow "U" gouge.

Remove the waste wood from the face of the tombstone.

Outline the top of the design using a shallow gouge.

This is the view of the piece part way through the carving process.

Shape the cat's tail back away from the front.

Outline the cat.

Remove the wood from the whole face of the tombstone as deep as you like.

Define all parts of the cat.

Carve away the wood from the face of the tombstone. The "Lon Gone" will be carved away also. This will be painted on. From here the project can be quickly finished by:
Shaping the pumpkin and carving the face as you wish.
Shaping the ghost and carving the face as you wish.
Shaping the cat's chin and ears but not the face.
Carving the back slightly if you wish.

Front view of the carving after it was cleaned up with a Foredom flexible shaft rotary tool. You can clean up your piece with a knife and sandpaper if you don't have access to a rotary tool.

Left front.

Back view. Note that I did carve very slightly on the back.

Right front.

Lon's Ghost finished project, fully painted. The detail of the cat will be highlighted in a separate photo. The pumpkin face was finished by darkening the eyes and adding black lines up the pumpkin to give the illusion of ridges. I painted little star symbols on Lon to give him some flair since he was such a big, white ghost. Copen Blue and Peyne's Gray were mixed to make the stars. I decorated the tombstone with little highlights to keep it from being too plain.

Back of Lon's Ghost.

Detail of the cat from Lon's Ghost. Oyster White was used on the tips of the ears, the end of the tail, around the eye shape, to create whiskers, and to define the tummy. A black dot and a slash of white gives the illusion of the eye. An orange collar not only helps define the separation of head and neck, but also gives a playful look. Black was swept on with a dry brush over the white tummy to look like fur. To dry brush, first dip the dry brush into a little paint. Use a paper towel to blot most of the paint off the brush. Use the brush with what little paint remains to sweep over the white tummy.

Detail of the face of Ghost With the Most. Copen Blue was used with some added white to make the eyes. A black dot adds life. The mouth was colored with diluted Peyne's Gray. I gave the ghost berry red plus white cheeks that came out a nice faded pink.

Details of the pumpkin in the ghost's hand. The eyes, nose, and mouth were filled in with yellow to give a hint of candlelight. A light wash of yellow was spread over the face to give a glint of candlelight. Black lines give the impression of ridges. The stem is green. Glitter adds an overall sparkle.

The tombstone, pumpkin, and bat from Ghost With the Most. Shading around the inner and outer edges of the tombstone make it stand out. Purple was used to tie in with the ghost's hatband.

Detail of the cat's face from Ghost With the Most. A light wash of gray and white lightened the face. The dry black brush was used to give the illusion of fur back across the edges. White dots were used for the eyes, eyebrows, whiskers, eyelashes, and mouth. A sliver of Wedgwood green highlighted the eyes. A little pink nose finished it off.

Details of the baby ghost. These are the same colors as in the rest of the piece. Stitch lines were added to the baby as they were on the big ghost. The baby's headband has white dots similar to those on the hat of the big ghost. These touches add detail and help tie the piece together.

Chapter Six
Painting the Pieces

Like Paul, I have never had formal decorative art training and have learned by trial and error. I had to learn by just jumping in and I encourage you to follow.

Much of the attractiveness of the finished product comes from the painting. The carved areas suggest certain treatments but the painter has a wide latitude to add details to make the creation come alive.

The design can be enhanced with plaids, dots, checks, swirls, and other highlight items. These details give the eye much to look at and enjoy. They can also help define scale in the carving as was done with the baby ghost's headband; the small dots help the baby look more childlike and small. Colors and patterns add interest and dimension.

I have found that shading also helps define the separation of areas. For example where the ghost's arm joins his body can be highlighted and separated with a little shading of a darker color. If you antique over the finished product this may do the job for you.

Choice of colors is critical. You may use exactly the colors we chose or you may venture out on your own. When you begin to do your own carving then your color choice *will* be critical. Trial and error is necessary sometimes but have a free spirit and try what comes to mind—after all you may come up with something new.

We chose to paint these projects with acrylic paints to take advantage of the fact that the acrylics are bright and playful. Other works of ours have been oil painted and you may find that technique described in our book *Carving and Painting an Heirloom Santa*, also from Schiffer.

The pieces received base coats of "White Lightning," a stain and sealer that gives a whitewashed look. This undercoat seals the wood so that the over layers of paint will not be absorbed and will appear more even. In the case of Lon's Ghost and the big ghost, I did not paint them any further since this white was satisfactory. The baby ghost was painted with Delta Oyster White.

For applying the "White Lightning," I used a 3/4" broad brush. For detail painting I used a #8 blender, a #12 blender, a 5 round, a 0 round, and a 5/0 detailer.

These pieces were sprayed lightly with Grumbacher Tuffilm matte finish spray to seal the pieces after base coating. The paints were Delta acrylic paints. A sparkle glaze was applied over the pieces after they were fully painted. This adds a glittery finish that helps catch the eye.

All paints are Delta. The cat, the bat, and the hat were painted with Black. The pumpkins are Orange. The pumpkin stem is Dark Jungle Green. The tombstone is Bridgeport Gray. The hatband is Vintage Wine.

Back side of the carving.

Lon's Ghost was painted with the same colors plus Berry Red for the hearts.

Back of the carving.

This is the finished piece with all of the details painted. The details will be highlighted in separate photos.

Back of the Ghost With The Most project.